A Concise Guide to Documentation:
MLA, APA, and Chicago

by Michael J. P. Larson

Minnesota State College – Southeast Technical

Winona, MN

A CreateSpace Book
North Charleston, SC

ISBN-13: 978-1469909028
ISBN-10: 1469909022

The writing of this book is due in large part to a sabbatical granted to the author by
Minnesota State College – Southeast Technical.

Table of Contents

Preface

The slim volume in your hands is meant to fill a narrow need but a tremendously common one. It is, as the title suggests, a concise guide to the three most popular documentation systems: MLA (Modern Language Association), APA (American Psychological Association), and CMS (Chicago Manual of Style). As a guide, it is a collection of the principles and format details for each system. As a concise guide, it is nothing more than that. In other words, this is not a text on how to conduct research or on how to write research papers. Neither does it provide style or format information that is not directly related to documentation. Rather, it is a singularly focused reference work on how to document sources precisely and correctly.

To my knowledge, there is not another book quite like it. In one volume, a writer (or budding writer) has the nuts and bolts of documentation technique for a wide variety of potential writing projects. MLA is the style generally preferred by the humanities disciplines: English (Composition, Literature, Linguistics), Speech and Rhetoric, Philosophy, Theology, Religion, Art and Architecture, Music, Dance, Theater, Classical Studies, Languages, and sometimes History. APA is the style generally preferred by the social sciences: Psychology, Sociology, Anthropology, Archeology, Geography, Economics, Business, Political Science, and sometimes History. APA style is also occasionally used in the natural sciences. CMS is the traditional documentation system able to accommodate all of the disciplines, whether in the humanities, the social sciences, or the natural sciences. Between the three systems, students ought to be able to handle the documentation portion of nearly any research assignment they may encounter in their academic careers.

While instructions for these three systems are readily available, in one form or another, on a multitude of Internet sites, those virtual locations cannot compete with the present text for ease of use or handiness, for portability, or for the pleasant sensation of having all the relevant information in one place—and quite literally at one's fingertips.

Finally, I must make mention of word processing programs that have a documentation feature built into the software. While impressive in its own right, this feature does not in fact show the writer *how* to document; rather, there are pop-up windows that prompt for segments of bibliographic information: the user fills in the blanks and—presto!—the in-text citation or the bibliographic page is conjured up on the screen in (allegedly) perfect format. An experienced writer, one who already knows how to document, can accomplish the same task (in probably less time) without making use of this gadget. What's more is that such a writer actually possesses a particular skill, a whole-picture understanding of the means by which credit is given where it is due and by which a reader may be directed to the relevant bibliographic information of a source. This humble but time-honored ability stands I think in favorable contrast to the act of merely handing over parceled bits of information to be processed and arranged by the machine. In the age of automatic spellcheckers and friendly grammar alerts, neither dictionaries nor grammar guides have become obsolete. It is my hope that this little book too will find an enduring place among writers' reference manuals.

~ Michael Larson, 2009

Introduction

There are two basic components to documentation: the *in-text citation* and the *bibliographic information*. The in-text citation is the indication, within the text of one's writing, that a source is being referenced. It provides some kind of link (e.g. an author's name, an article title, a note number) to the bibliographic information, which is located at the end of the written piece (or in a footnote). The bibliographic information, a separate entry for each source, contains the pertinent publication details—author, title, publisher, date, etc.—so that a reader may refer to the source for verification, for further study, or for a better understanding of context.

Part One of this book focuses on in-text citation, first explaining the general principles as they pertain to all three systems—Modern Language Association (MLA), American Psychological Association (APA), and Chicago Manual of Style (CMS)—and then providing examples of various types of in-text citations, specific to each system. **Part Two** adheres to the same pattern—general principles followed by specific examples—applied this time to bibliographic citations, including sample completed bibliographic pages for each of the three systems. In both parts of the text, the goal is to show what one needs to know in order to document properly the vast majority of sources. In other words, the sample in-text and bibliographic citations are not meant to be exhaustive of every documentation challenge that could conceivably arise (each of the systems has its own thick guidebook to fulfill that purpose). Rather, this text seeks to provide the basic principles and the most common examples, which may account for perhaps 90% or more of the documentation precisions required of most students in their academic careers. And in those rare instances where they need to document an unusual type of source not covered here, then they may be guided in most cases by an understanding of the principles behind documentation in general and behind each of the three systems in particular.

Finally, there is also an **Appendix**, directing the reader to more comprehensive resources for research and documentation.

.

Part One: In-Text Citation

General Principles

1. Avoiding Plagiarism

   Plagiarism is the presentation of another's words or ideas as if they are your own. It is considered a serious academic offense. An awareness, then, of how to avoid it is the first principle in the study of documentation.

The Words of Others

   Whenever you wish to capture in your own writing the exact wording of any source,[1] you must do two things: 1) indicate which words belong to someone else, and 2) make an in-text citation. The words of others are indicated either by quotation marks around them or by an exaggerated indentation of the entire block of quoted words. Samples of both methods will appear in the next chapter. The format for in-text citations varies from one documentation system to another. Samples of MLA, APA, and CMS systems will be provided throughout the text.

The Ideas of Others

   Even if you do not wish to use the exact wording of a source, you may wish to paraphrase or summarize the source material because the idea contained therein is of use to you in the writing of your paper. In this case, even though you are not using the source's actual wording, you must still include an in-text citation in order to avoid plagiarism.

---

[1] Here the word, "source," refers to anything or anyone consulted in the research process, whether written or spoken, whether textual or visual.

Paraphrasing is the restating of the source material in roughly the same amount of space but with significantly different word choices and sentence structure. If the wording and/or the sentence structure is too close to that of the original source, then you run the risk of plagiarism (even if you include an in-text citation) because you give the appearance that the phrasing itself is yours when in fact it is heavily reliant on the source.

Summarizing is the condensing of source material into a smaller space. A paragraph might be condensed into a single sentence; an article or chapter might be condensed into a single paragraph. In summary, key points are mentioned, but details are left out. As with a paraphrase, a summary must not use wording from the original source and must include an in-text citation for that source.

Common Knowledge

The only time you do not need to document source material in your paper is when you are paraphrasing or summarizing an idea or fact that is already commonly known or at least easily verifiable in multiple sources. Verbatim quotations—even if they *are* of common knowledge—do need an in-text citation; the only exceptions to this would be common sayings or proverbs that have become a part of popular culture and are therefore no longer attributed to the originator of the wording.

To repeat, if the fact or idea you are referencing can be found easily in a number of different sources, then it is probably common knowledge and does not require documentation. If, however, you are unsure about whether a piece of information is common knowledge or not, it is better to err on the side of safety and cite it.

2. Appropriating Credit

The flip side of avoiding plagiarism is giving credit where credit is due. The ideas of another person, as well as the particular way those ideas are phrased, are considered intellectual property. As such, it is only a matter of justice to identify the true owner of those words and/or ideas.

From a practical point of view, the appropriation of credit also provides readers with the means by which they can locate the source—perhaps to verify the accuracy of the citation, perhaps to better understand the context of the source material, perhaps to study the matter further.

3. Building Credibility

A third principle behind accurate documentation is one of its effects: the building of credibility. Those who document accurately and thoroughly are simply more credible as writers than those who do not. The very presence of careful documentation, then, works to build and sustain the ethos[2] of the writer and thereby makes the reader more receptive to the writer's message.

4. Signal Phrases

The term, "signal phrase," refers to the optional practice of naming your source—and any additional description of that source—*within* the actual text of your writing, as opposed to doing so only in a parenthetical or numbered citation. Although there are some subtle distinctions between the three systems—MLA, APA, and CMS—as to how signal phrases are handled, the basic principles are essentially the same.

Introducing a Source

The first time your paper makes reference to a particular source, it is usually a good idea to state the source's full name, with titles if appropriate, as well as any important credentials, especially as those credentials come to bear on the point you are trying to make at that juncture in the paper. Consider the following:

Miriam Turner, Director of the River Arts Institute, agrees that funding cuts ...

It should be noted that the APA recommends last-name-only even for the first use of a source, especially when that source happens to be, as is often the case in the social sciences, the published results of a particular study, which may have included several researchers, as follows:

Ames, Hanson, Laird, and Wiley (2001) conclude ...

Subsequent References to a Source

After the first reference to a source, any subsequent references to the same source need only include the last name in the signal phrase, as follows:

While others in the arts community argue for higher taxes, Turner counters ...

---

[2] *Ethos* is an Aristotelian term from rhetoric. In the case of written rhetoric, it refers to the reader's perception of the writer—specifically as regards the writer's intelligence, character, and good will.

Verbs

As part of a signal phrase, you must choose a verb to express the source's act of communication. For instance, *Harold Smith* **says** *that the species is endangered.* Notice that the verb, "says," is in the present tense. This tells us that Mr. Smith's words exist *in the present* in some kind of published text. Any time you are referring to the words or ideas of an existing text, you should use the simple present tense when referring to it. However, if you are describing what an individual or a particular group of researchers *did*, as opposed to what they wrote, then the simple past tense would be more appropriate: *Henderson and Gray* **conducted** *an experiment in 1962.*

Aside from tense, there is also the matter of verb choice. Although the quiet verb, *says*, is a safe and reliable choice, mixing up the signal-phrase verbs throughout a piece of writing will add variety, helping the overall flow while avoiding monotony. The following is a list of some common alternatives—each with slightly different connotative meaning—for signal-phrase verbs, expressed in singular, present-tense form:

says	reports	insists	advises	communicates
notes	writes	clarifies	deduces	divulges
argues	states	explains	implies	asks
asserts	points out	establishes	reasons	admits
relates	discloses	observes	concludes	puzzles
suggests	counters	announces	proposes	warns

5. Necessary Elements

If the purpose of an in-text citation is to point the reader to a location with more detailed bibliographic information, then there are certain necessary elements to accomplish this task, no matter which system of documentation is being used. Specific examples for each system will appear in the next chapter.

MLA

The MLA system requires two components to the in-text citation:

- Source surname
- Page number (if available)

The source surname will serve as the link to the MLA "Works Cited" page, appearing at the end of a paper. Because the Works Cited page is organized alphabetically by surname, the reader will be easily able to find the bibliographic details for the source in question. If the source has page numbers, then the specific page number(s) should be included in the in-text citation as well. Page numbers always go in parentheses right after the source material, whereas the source surname may go in the signal phrase, as discussed in #4 above, or if not there, then in the parentheses with the page number(s).

APA

The APA system also requires two components for any in-text citation and an additional third component when there is a direct quotation involved:

- Source surname
- Four-digit year of publication
- Page number (if direct quotation)

Like the MLA "Works Cited" page, the APA "References" page is organized alphabetically by surname, so the in-text citation must include that surname as a means of connecting the source material to the detailed bibliographic information at the end of the paper. Also as with MLA style, the source's surname may be included either in the signal phrase or in a parenthetical citation right after the source material is referenced in the paper.

Unlike the MLA, however, the APA requires in the in-text citation a four-digit year indicating the source's date of publication. Although this date may be included in the signal phrase, it is much more commonly placed in parentheses right after the source is named.

The APA in-text citation *requires* a page number *only* in the case of a direct quotation. It stands to reason, however, that even paraphrases or summaries might benefit from the presence of a page number indicating the exact location of the referenced material, especially if the source is lengthy, such as a book or a very long article.

Finally, it should be noted that the APA makes a distinction between published and private sources. Personal interviews and private written correspondence (e.g. via postal or electronic mail) are not listed on the "References" page because they are, by and large, inaccessible to a reader. Therefore, the complete bibliographic information for those types of sources is given in the in-text citation: initial for first name, followed by surname, followed by the designation "personal communication," followed by the exact date (e.g. J. Frank, personal communication, July 12, 2004).

CMS

The Chicago Manual of Style endorses two basic methods of documentation: a name-and-date method, which is similar in principle to the APA style, and a numbered note method, which is the one that this present text will be exemplifying whenever it uses the acronym, "CMS."

The CMS system of in-text documentation is least intrusive to the text of a paper because all that is required at the place where a source is being referenced is a simple note number in superscript (i.e. raised a half line from the rest of the text). This number points the reader to an identically numbered footnote at the bottom of that same page or endnote at the end of the paper; in either case, the bibliographic information for that source is contained in that note. Note numbers start with the Arabic numeral, "1," and advance sequentially throughout the paper.

Of course, it is permissible—even advantageous—to name your source and relevant credentials in a signal phrase (as discussed above in #4); it's just that nothing more than a note number is actually *required* for the in-text portion of CMS documentation.

6. Marking Source Boundaries

When you do make reference to a source, it must be clear to your reader where the source's words and/or ideas begin and end.

Single Sentence

When the source material being referenced is contained in a single sentence, there is little confusion. The source is typically named in a signal phrase, and the sentence is followed by a parenthetical citation (MLA and APA) or a note number (CMS). Thus the reader can see clearly where the source material begins and ends.

Multiple Sentences

If a summary or paraphrase takes two or more sentences, it can be difficult sometimes for the reader to see the boundaries of the source material. The endpoint should be clear—either a parenthetical citation or a note number—but the starting point can be a little ambiguous. It is essential in these cases that the writer use a signal phrase in the first sentence in order to mark the beginning of the reference to the source. As discussed in #4, this will usually mean naming the source, but it could also be marked by a reference to the title of the work rather than the author (who would then have to be named in the parenthetical citation that follows). In any case, if the writer marks the first sentence with a signal phrase and the end of the last sentence with a parenthetical citation or note number, then a kind of frame around the source material is created, and the reader is able to see clear separation between the ideas of the writer and those of the writer's sources.

<u>Quotations</u>

As with the single-sentence reference, quotations provide an easy visual boundary for the reader to identify what is and is not source material. Samples of quotations and their in-text citations will follow in the next chapter, but first, here are some general principles related to their use:

i.   Short quotations are indicated by quotation marks (" "). MLA defines *short* as 4 lines of text or less. APA defines it as 40 words or less. CMS defines it as less than 100 words or less than 8 lines, provided the quoted material comprises not more than one paragraph of the original source.

ii.   Long quotations are indicated by extra indentation (10 spaces, MLA and CMS; 5 spaces, APA), and quotation marks are not used. This is called a "block quotation." MLA defines *long* as more than 4 lines of text. APA defines it as more than 40 words. CMS defines it as any one of the following: 100 words or more, more than 8 lines, or material from more than one paragraph of the original source.

iii.   Sometimes a quotation from a source will include the source's use of quotation marks as well. In that case, if the overall quotation is short, use the apostrophe mark (' ') to indicate interior quotation marks. In a block quotation, on the other hand, quotation marks should simply be left as they appear in the original.

iv.   When you quote a source, the words and punctuation must appear exactly as they do in the original. You are not free to make even slight changes (excepting the quotation mark change described above) without indication to the reader. Brackets [ ] are used to show any authorial additions or substitutions inside the quoted material. In MLA format, brackets are also used to show deletions of any portion of the original quotation. When using brackets for this purpose, the ellipsis mark is used, as follows: […]. Neither APA nor CMS requires the use of brackets here—just the ellipsis mark.

In-text Examples

The examples that follow are invented to represent a variety of in-text citation situations. Since documentation relies at its most basic level on the identification of authors (or other sources[3]), the first several example groupings are organized by various author possibilities. In each case there are three tables displaying first an initial reference to a source as it might first appear in a paper, then subsequent references with and without the use of a signal phrase. After these "author" tables are some other classifications of in-text citations: those having to do with citing multiple sentences and those for citing quotations. The example groupings proceed sequentially as follows:

1. One Author
2. Two Authors
3. Three Authors
4. More than Three Authors
5. Corporate Author
6. Unknown Author
7. Multiple-Sentence Citations
8. Short Quotations
9. Long Quotations
10. Quotations within Source Passages

---

[3] Not all sources are verbal (a painting, for instance); thus the term, "author," does not always apply, though it does in the vast majority of cases.

1. One Author

   a. Initial Reference

MLA	Samuel Hunt, Professor of Physics at Franklin College, notes that both heliocentrism and geocentrism are mathematically viable (17).
APA	S. Hunt (2003), Professor of Physics at Franklin College, notes that both heliocentrism and geocentrism are mathematically viable (p. 17). [Note: inclusion of page number(s) is *optional* for APA when the reference is not a direct quotation.]
CMS	Samuel Hunt, Professor of Physics at Franklin College, notes that both heliocentrism and geocentrism are mathematically viable.[1]

   b. Subsequent Reference, author named in signal phrase

MLA	Hunt describes the prevailing view as overconfident (19).
APA	Hunt (2003) describes the prevailing view as overconfident.
CMS	Hunt describes the prevailing view as overconfident.[2]

   c. Subsequent Reference, author not named in signal phrase

MLA	The prevailing view has been described as overconfident (Hunt 19).
APA	The prevailing view has been described as overconfident (Hunt, 2003).
CMS	The prevailing view has been described as overconfident.[2]

2. Two Authors

    a. Initial Reference

MLA	Researchers Justin Reid and Anthony Gibbons discovered that most people are unwilling to make a choice in such circumstances (74 – 81).
APA	Reid and Gibbons (1998) discovered that most people are unwilling to make a choice in such circumstances (pp. 74 – 81). [Note: inclusion of page number(s) is *optional* for APA when the reference is not a direct quotation.]
CMS	Researchers Justin Reid and Anthony Gibbons discovered that most people are unwilling to make a choice in such circumstances.[3]

    b. Subsequent Reference, authors named in signal phrase

MLA	According to Reid and Gibbons, the anxiety extends across all age groups (78).
APA	According to Reid and Gibbons (1998), the anxiety extends across all age groups.
CMS	According to Reid and Gibbons, the anxiety extends across all age groups.[4]

    c. Subsequent Reference, authors not named in signal phrase

MLA	The anxiety extends across all age groups (Reid and Gibbons 78).
APA	The anxiety extends across all age groups (Reid & Gibbons, 1998).
CMS	The anxiety extends across all age groups.[4]

3. Three Authors

    a. Initial Reference

MLA	John Hand, Mary Burbitz, and Susan Welch argue that the early reports of Townsend's youth were strongly biased (21).
APA	Hand, Burbitz, and Welch (1989) argue that the early reports of Townsend's youth were strongly biased (p. 21). [Note: inclusion of page number(s) is *optional* for APA when the reference is not a direct quotation.]
CMS	John Hand, Mary Burbitz, and Susan Welch argue that the early reports of Townsend's youth were strongly biased.[5]

    b. Subsequent Reference, authors named in signal phrase

MLA	Hand, Burbitz, and Welch assert that Miles Townsend was actually of noble birth (84-85).
APA	Hand et al. (1989) assert that Miles Townsend was actually of noble birth.
CMS	Hand, Burbitz, and Welch assert that Miles Townsend was actually of noble birth. [6]

    c. Subsequent Reference, authors not named in signal phrase

MLA	But apparently Miles Townsend was actually of noble birth (Hand, Burbitz, and Welch 84-85).
APA	But apparently Miles Townsend was actually of noble birth (Hand et al., 1989).
CMS	But apparently Miles Townsend was actually of noble birth.[6]

4. More than Three Authors

   a. Initial Reference

MLA	Michael Hammerstand et al. suggest in the book, *Starlight*, that these waves could be much younger than previously thought (231).
APA	Hammerstand et al. (2006) suggest in the book, *Starlight*, that these waves could be much younger than previously thought. [Note: The example here applies to a work of 6 or more authors. If there were 4 or 5 authors, it would be handled the same as with 3 authors (see the prior example).]
CMS	Michael Hammerstand et al. suggest in the book, *Starlight*, that these waves could be much younger than previously thought.[7]

   b. Subsequent Reference, authors named in signal phrase

MLA	Hammerstand et al. are convinced that time travel remains intrinsically impossible (314).
APA	Hammerstand et al. (2006) are convinced that time travel remains intrinsically impossible.
CMS	Hammerstand et al. are convinced that time travel remains intrinsically impossible.[8]

   c. Subsequent Reference, authors not named in signal phrase

MLA	Time travel remains intrinsically impossible (Hammerstand et al. 314).
APA	Time travel remains intrinsically impossible (Hammerstand et al., 2006).
CMS	Time travel remains intrinsically impossible.[8]

5. Corporate Author

A corporate author refers to any publication put out by a corporate or sponsoring organization without naming any individual authors. In that case, it is the organization itself that is considered to be the author and is therefore the link to the bibliographic information in both MLA and APA systems. Although it is permissible for subsequent references to continue naming the organizational author in a signal phrase, parenthetical references are more common, especially when the organization's name is a long one.

a. Initial Reference

MLA	The Kensington Historical Society claims that the settlement was nearly wiped out in 1891 by a raging fire (12).
APA	The Kensington Historical Society (KHS, 1972) claims that the settlement was nearly wiped out in 1891 by a raging fire. [Note: an acronym (e.g. *KHS*) is only needed in the initial reference if there will also be subsequent references to the organizational author.]
CMS	The Kensington Historical Society claims that the settlement was nearly wiped out in 1891 by a raging fire.[9]

b. Subsequent Reference

MLA	In the end, the gold rush was both boom and bust for the fledgling community (Kensington Hist. Soc. 17-18).
APA	In the end, the gold rush was both boom and bust for the fledgling community (KHS, 1972, pp. 17-18). [Note: inclusion of page number(s) is *optional* for APA when the reference is not a direct quotation.]
CMS	In the end, the gold rush was both boom and bust for the fledgling community.[10]

6. Unknown (or Anonymous) Author

If the author of a source is unknown, the next means of source identification is the title of the work.

a. Author Unknown, Title Given in Signal Phrase

MLA	"A Soldier's Diary from the Great War" recounts the care with which the operation was planned (27).
APA	"A soldier's diary from the great war" (1954) recounts the care with which the operation was planned.
CMS	"A Soldier's Diary from the Great War" recounts the care with which the operation was planned.[11]

b. Author Unknown, No Title Given in Signal Phrase

MLA	There is evidence, though, that the operation was planned with great care ("Soldier's Diary…" 27).
APA	There is evidence, though, that the operation was planned with great care ("Soldier's diary," 1954).
CMS	There is evidence, though, that the operation was planned with great care.[11]

c. Author Named as "Anonymous"

MLA	The despair is clear in the anonymous poem, "The Willow's Grasp" (271).
APA	The despair is clear in the poem, "The Willow's Grasp" (Anonymous, 1943).
CMS	The despair is clear in the anonymous poem, "The Willow's Grasp."[12]

7. Multiple-Sentence Citations

A paraphrase or summary that extends beyond one sentence needs some kind of frame, a way to mark both the beginning and the end of the source material. The examples in the following table each accomplish this by naming the source in a signal phrase at the start and by the indication of a page or note number at the finish. The reader is then able to deduce that all of the information in between comes from that source—in this case, "John Glass"—by way of the paraphrase/summary.

MLA	John Glass, Director of the River Research Institute, explains that a number of aquatic biologists had already noticed the dramatic change in shoreline vegetation. The problem was that nobody could figure out the cause. To compound the problem, funding had been cut drastically in the prior year, so the research dollars simply weren't there (8).
APA	John Glass (2005), Director of the River Research Institute, explains that a number of aquatic biologists had already noticed the dramatic change in shoreline vegetation. The problem was that nobody could figure out the cause. To compound the problem, funding had been cut drastically in the prior year, so the research dollars simply weren't there (p. 8). [Note: Although a page number is not required here for APA, it is an excellent method of creating an endpoint for this multi-sentence citation.]
CMS	John Glass, Director of the River Research Institute, explains that a number of aquatic biologists had already noticed the dramatic change in shoreline vegetation. The problem was that nobody could figure out the cause. To compound the problem, funding had been cut drastically in the prior year, so the research dollars simply weren't there.[13]

As the above examples illustrate, the parenthetical page number works very well to mark the end of a multi-sentence paraphrase or summary. If your source is a website, however, then you likely will not have a page number to work with. In that case, the frame can be created by another means. For instance, at the beginning of the first sentence, the website itself can be named, and the end of the multi-sentence reference can then be marked by a parenthetical citation of the author last name (and date, in the case of APA) for both MLA and APA styles.

8. Short Quotations

MLA = 4 lines of text or less
APA = 40 words or less
CMS = 8 lines of text or less, 100 words or less, and not more than 1 source paragraph

   a. Source Named after Quotation

MLA	"We're going to see a return to the gold standard, all around the globe, as a pendulum-swing reaction to loose monetary policy," says Martin Gross, of Barton Trends Research (47).
APA	"We're going to see a return to the gold standard, all around the globe, as a pendulum-swing reaction to loose monetary policy," says Martin Gross (2009, p. 47), of Barton Trends Research.
CMS	"We're going to see a return to the gold standard, all around the globe, as a pendulum-swing reaction to loose monetary policy,"[14] says Martin Gross, of Barton Trends Research.

   b. Source Named before Quotation

MLA	Nancy Willet and Bill Bray report, "Almost two-thirds of the adult population have never contacted a state legislator" (9).
APA	Willet and Bray (2001) report, "Almost two-thirds of the adult population have never contacted a state legislator" (p. 9).
CMS	Nancy Willet and Bill Bray report, "Almost two-thirds of the adult population have never contacted a state legislator."[15]

9. Long Quotations

MLA = more than 4 lines of text
APA = more than 40 words
CMS = more than 8 lines of text, more than 100 words, or more than 1 source paragraph

Long quotations require an introductory sentence before the quotation itself is set apart from the rest of the text by way of indentation (10 spaces for MLA and CMS; 5 spaces for APA). Although the examples here are in single-spacing, *block quotations in your paper should double-spaced throughout*, just like the rest of your text, and quotation marks should not be used.

MLA	In his essay, *50 Kings*, Ross Hildebrandt makes an interesting case for monarchy over democracy: A monarch, unlike a president, is not bound to popular opinion. While he may take the will of the people into consideration, he is free to make an unpopular decision if he believes it to be for the long-term good of the country, which is under his paternal care. A president, on the other hand, must always be concerned about the next election and the political jockeying that must go on endlessly in a democracy and that changes over every few years. Which brings up another point: while hereditary monarchies have at least the potential for long-term leadership stability—decades, if not generations, of a consistent style and outlook—democracies are inherently unstable because every election forces opposing factions to attempt to divide and conquer the general population. (8)
APA	In his essay, *50 Kings*, Ross Hildebrandt (2008) makes an interesting case for monarchy over democracy: A monarch, unlike a president, is not bound to popular opinion. While he may take the will of the people into consideration, he is free to make an unpopular decision if he believes it to be for the long-term good of the country, which is under his paternal care. A president, on the other hand, must always be concerned about the next election and the political jockeying that must go on endlessly in a democracy and that changes over every few years. Which brings up another point: while hereditary monarchies have at least the potential for long-term leadership stability—decades, if not generations, of a consistent style and outlook—democracies are inherently unstable because every election forces opposing factions to attempt to divide and conquer the general population. (p. 8)
CMS	In his essay, *50 Kings*, Ross Hildebrandt makes an interesting case for monarchy over democracy: A monarch, unlike a president, is not bound to popular opinion. While he may take the will of the people into consideration, he is free to make an unpopular decision if he believes it to be for the long-term good of the country, which is under his paternal care. A president, on the other hand, must always be concerned about the next election and the political jockeying that must go on endlessly in a democracy and that changes over every few years. Which brings up another point: while hereditary monarchies have at least the potential for long-term leadership stability—decades, if not generations, of a consistent style and outlook—democracies are inherently unstable because every election forces opposing factions to attempt to divide and conquer the general population.[16]

10. Quotations within Source Passages

Sometimes there is the need to quote something that is already within quotation marks as it stands in the original source—perhaps because it is a title or a word emphasized for its own sake. Other times it is because another source is being quoted within your source. The following examples illustrate this circumstance.

a. Quotations within Quotations

MLA	As Roberts reminds us, "Sam Harrelson was intent on gaining command. He even wrote in his diary, 'I will let nothing stand in the way of my objective'" (84). [Here the source is Roberts (not Harrelson), and he has been named in a signal phrase. Furthermore, by the use of the apostrophe marks, Harrelson's words are clearly distinguished from those of Roberts. In block quotations, regular quotation marks would be used (instead of the apostrophe marks) to set off internal quotations.]
APA	As Roberts (1992) reminds us, "Sam Harrelson was intent on gaining command. He even wrote in his diary, 'I will let nothing stand in the way of my objective'" (p. 84).
CMS	As Roberts reminds us, "Sam Harrelson was intent on gaining command. He even wrote in his diary, 'I will let nothing stand in the way of my objective.'"[17]

b. Secondary Source Quotation *without* the Primary Source in Signal Phrase

MLA	As Sheriff Talbert has said, "The water supply has been compromised, whether by natural causes or by criminal activity" (qtd. in Hutchins A12).
APA	As Sheriff Talbert has said, "The water supply has been compromised, whether by natural causes or by criminal activity" (cited in Hutchins, 2007, p. A12).
CMS	As Sheriff Talbert has said, "The water supply has been compromised, whether by natural causes or by criminal activity."[18]

Part Two: Bibliographic Citation

General Principles

Bibliographic citations are the other half of the documentation equation. Every in-text citation should point the reader to a particular bibliographic citation, where precise publication information can be found. What follows in this section are a few general principles about how this information is arranged and formatted. In the next section are numerous examples of common types of sources for each of the three systems—MLA, APA, and CMS.

1. Nomenclature, Location, and Spacing

   In MLA style, the sheet on which you arrange the bibliographic information for your sources is added to the end of your paper and is called the "Works Cited" page. In APA style, it is called the "References" page and is also added to the end of the paper. In both MLA and APA styles, double spacing is maintained throughout the bibliographic page, both between and within individual citations.

   In CMS style, there are two options: footnotes or endnotes. If footnotes are used, the bibliographic information appears, single-spaced, at the bottom of each page where sources are used, and there is no special title given to the notes themselves. If endnotes are used, then as with MLA and APA, a page with double spacing throughout is added to the end of the paper and titled simply, "Notes."

2. Arrangement

In both MLA and APA styles, bibliographic citations are keyed in their arrangement by author last name, if available, and by the first word in the title (excluding prepositions and articles) when the author is unknown. If there is more than one author of a single source, then the alphabetizer is the first author named in the source itself. Because they are alphabetized by author last name, both MLA and APA make the first line of the bibliographic entry flush with the left margin of the paper. Each subsequent line (if there are any) of an individual entry is then indented 5 spaces.

In CMS style, whether footnotes or endnotes, the bibliographic citations are simply arranged sequentially according to the Arabic numerals that mark the in-text citations. The first line in a CMS note is indented 5 spaces, and any subsequent lines for a particular note are flush with the left margin.

3. Division of Bibliographic Information and Related Format Issues

A bibliographic citation can be divided into three basic parts: author name, title of work, and publishing information.

Author Name

Since the very purpose of documentation is to give credit where it is due, the author's name is the most important piece of a bibliographic citation. And as the first piece of information in any given citation, it is also the means by which MLA and APA entries are arranged on the page, in inverted order—last name first; CMS, on the other hand, since it is sequenced by numbers and not names, presents the author name as we normally perceive it: first name followed by last name. Both first and last name (and middle name or initial when it is available) are given for MLA and CMS styles, whereas APA style gives only first initial (and middle initial when it is available) along with the last name.

Title of Work

While the author name gives the reader the *who* of the source, the title of the work names the *what*.

i.   Capitalization
     MLA and CMS styles capitalize the first letter of the first word in a title and the first letter of all significant words thereafter (typically excluding prepositions, conjunctions, and articles). APA, however, capitalizes only the

first letter of the first word of the title. The rest of the letters are lower case, excepting, of course, the first letter of any proper noun. An exception to this within the APA system is the titles of periodicals, which are capitalized in the traditional style, as exemplified by MLA and CMS.

    ii.   Typographical Techniques

        a. *For stand-alone sources*: Any work that exists on its own and not as part of a larger work is considered a stand-alone source (e.g. books, periodicals, websites, CDs, etc.). CMS indicates this kind of source with either italics or underlining, whereas MLA and APA allow italics only.

        b. *For a segment of a larger work*: Many sources are not published as individual entities but as a part of something larger (e.g. a forward or a single chapter in a book, an article in a periodical, an article on a website, a particular song on a CD, etc.). In CMS and MLA, these titles are indicated by the use of quotation marks, whereas in APA, nothing is done to the text: no underlining, no italics, no quotation marks.

Publishing Information

Publisher information is the most varied aspect of bibliographic citations, and there are many subtle (and some not so subtle) differences between the three systems. These will be exemplified in the next section, but a brief discussion of the basic components is available here.

    i.   Books

When the source being referenced is a book, publishing information always includes the name of the publisher, the city wherein the publisher resides, and the year of publication. Other information attached to some sources are the edition number (if beyond the first edition), series title, editor name(s) (if different than the "author name"), translator name, etc.. Also, in the CMS system, since page number(s) are not given in the in-text citation, they are given in each bibliographic note and correspond to the specific location within the source that is being referenced at the place of the corresponding in-text note number. In addition, MLA indicates whether the researcher is using a print copy or an online version of the book.

    ii.   Periodicals

When the source being referenced is an article or other short piece within the pages of a magazine or journal or newspaper, the publishing information always includes the title of the periodical, issue date or volume information, including a four-digit year, and page numbers for the article itself. In CMS, though, only the page number to which the particular note is referring need be included. MLA also indicates whether the researcher is using a print copy or an online version of the periodical, including one retrieved from a library database service.

iii.   Electronic Sources

There are many idiosyncrasies among the three systems in formatting bibliographic citations for electronic sources. Those will be exemplified in the next section, but in general, in addition to an author name and a specific title, electronic-source citations include the name of the website (or database service), the name of a sponsoring organization (if available), date of publication or update (if available), a date of retrieval, and—in some cases—a URL address or a Digital Object Identifier.

iv.   Other Sources

Other sources include digital media, live performances, speeches, lectures, artwork, etc.. The same principles apply to these as to other types of sources. Basically, the citation should describe who did what (author/artist name and title of work) and where it can be found, or at least when it happened (publishing or event information). Some examples of the more common types will follow in the next section.

4. CMS Subsequent Notes Referring to Same Author

Unlike MLA and APA styles, wherein each source is listed only once on the Works Cited or References page, there is a numbered CMS note to correspond to *every* in-text citation, even if it refers to an author already named. Consequently, CMS has a shortened means for these subsequent notes, as follows:

Initial note:

1. William Hughes, *The Fox in the Sage* (Boston: Brookes Limited, 1974), 94.

Subsequent, immediately following, same source page:

2. Ibid.

Subsequent, immediately following, different source page:

    2.   Ibid., 103.

Subsequent, but not immediately following:

    9.   Hughes, 103.

Bibliographic Citation Examples

The 40 examples that follow are invented to illustrate a variety of common bibliographic citations. No attempt has been made to list every conceivable type of source; nevertheless, these examples ought to account for the great majority of sources you might encounter. And for the occasional rarity, you cannot go far astray by simply applying the same general principles present in the citation of more common sources. Remember, the reader's basic question is this: *Who said what, and where can I find it?* Following is the sequence of source types used to illustrate each system's method of formatting an answer to that question.[4]

Author Naming Conventions

1. One Author
2. Two or Three Authors
3. More than Three Authors
4. Anonymous Author
5. Multiple Works by the Same Author

Print Books

6. Basic
7. Editor as Main Author
8. Author with Editor
9. Author with Translator

---

[4] Note that all the example citations are double-spaced, as they would appear in a bibliographic page at the end of a paper. If you were to use CMS, footnotes style, then the entries would be at the bottom of each page where they are used, and single spaced. All other formatting details would remain the same.

10. Individual Work in an Anthology
11. Guest Author Preface, Forward, Introduction, etc.
12. Edition beyond First
13. Book within Multivolume Set
14. Reference Work: Encyclopedia or Dictionary
15. Corporate Author
16. Sacred Text

Print Periodicals

17. Basic Journal
18. Basic Magazine
19. Newsletter
20. Basic Newspaper
21. Interview
22. Reviews
23. Editorial
24. Letter to the Editor

Online Sources

25. Online Book
26. Online-Periodical Article
27. Article from a Database
28. Website
29. Posting to a Discussion Board
30. Comment to a Blog Posting

Other Sources

31. Public Documents
32. Film
33. Audio Recording
34. Television Program
35. Radio Program
36. Public Address
37. Live Performance
38. Artwork
39. Personal Interview
40. Personal Correspondence

Author Naming Conventions

In this section, complete citations are not given. Rather, the examples are meant to show the differences between the three systems only with regard to how each handles author names.

1. One Author

MLA	Sanchez, Cecilia.
APA	Sanchez, C.
CMS	8. Cecilia Sanchez,

2. Two or Three Authors

MLA	Farr, Helga T., and Mitch Wilson. [For three authors, the same format is followed but with the "and" coming between the second and the third.]
APA	Farr, H. T., & Wilson, M. [For three authors, the same format is followed but with the ampersand (&) coming between the second and the third.]
CMS	9. Helga T. Farr and Mitch Wilson, [For three authors, as follows: 2. Helga T. Farr, Mitch Wilson, and Rhonda Freeze,]

3. More than Three Authors

MLA	Akkopia, Amir, et al.
APA	Akkopia, A., Strehl, R., Mann, P., Erickson, J., Hess, F., Jewel, K., et al. [APA names all authors up to six before indicating that there are more who are unnamed.]
CMS	4. Amir Akkopia et al.,

4. Anonymous (or Unknown) Author

MLA	"The Gathering Gloom." [When the author is unknown, even if named as "anonymous," MLA defaults to the title of the work as the alphabetizer—in this case, the word, "Gathering," because the article, "The," would be ignored.]
APA	Anonymous. [If the author is listed in the source itself as "anonymous," then APA uses that designation in place of an author's name. Otherwise, APA resorts to the title of the work (as with MLA).]
CMS	5. "The Gathering Gloom," [Like the MLA, CMS uses title of the work as the first portion of a note entry when the author is unknown.]

5. Multiple Works by the Same Author

MLA	Wenzl, Alice. "Blueprint for Revolution." ---. "Reinterpreting 1789." [Note that the title of the work determines the order.]
APA	Wenzl, A. (2003). Wenzl, A. (2006). [Note that the year of publication determines the order.]
CMS	6. Alice Wenzl, "Reinterpreting 1789," 17. Alice Wenzl, "Blueprint for Revolution," [Note that CMS notes are not alphabetized but sequenced by number in the order that they appear in the text.]

This section exemplifies the format for physical books, stand-alone publications you can hold in your hand, whether a pamphlet of few pages or a multi-volume encyclopedia or any size in between. Note that for publisher names, typically only the first key identifying word is used. Also note that CMS indicates page number (when available) in its bibliographic notes.

6. Basic

MLA	Coles, Jack. *The End of Modernity*. New York: Blackstone, 1999. Print.
APA	Coles, J. (1999). *The end of modernity*. New York: Blackstone.
CMS	1. Jack Coles, *The End of Modernity* (New York: Blackstone, 1999), 31. [Initial reference. See General Principles, #4, for subsequent reference patterns.]

7. Editor as Main Author

MLA	Hartston, John A., ed. *Anonymous Diaries of WWI*. London: Edgecombe, 1987. Print.
APA	Hartston, J. A. (Ed.). (1987). *Anonymous diaries of WWI*. London: Edgecombe.
CMS	2. John A. Hartston, ed., *Anonymous Diaries of WWI* (London: Edgecombe, 1987), 47. [Initial reference. See General Principles, #4, for subsequent reference patterns.]

8. Author with Editor

MLA	Sauger, Mary. *Collected Essays of Mary Sauger*. Ed. Cheryl Berrins. New York: Crest, 1984. Print.
APA	Sauger, M. (1984). In C. Berrins (Ed.), *Collected essays of Mary Sauger*. New York: Crest.
CMS	3. Mary Sauger, *Collected Essays of Mary Sauger*, ed. Cheryl Berrins (New York: Crest, 1984), 72. [Initial reference. See General Principles, #4, for subsequent reference patterns.]

9. Author with Translator

MLA	Diaz, Juan. *Brazilian Gemstones*. Trans. Lyle Welter. New York: Holt-Lewis, 1939. Print.
APA	Diaz, J. (1939). *Brazilian gemstones* (L. Welter, Trans.). New York: Holt-Lewis.
CMS	4. Juan Diaz, *Brazilian Gemstones*, trans. Lyle Welter (New York: Holt-Lewis, 1939), 344. [Initial reference. See General Principles, #4, for subsequent reference patterns.]

10. Individual Work in an Anthology

MLA	Martin, Frank. "Wheat and Rye." *Earth Poems*. Ed. Louise J. Cowley. North Branch, TX: Freeman UP, 2004. Print.
APA	Martin, F. (2004). Wheat and rye. In L. J. Cowley (Ed.), *Earth poems* (pp. 21-22). North Branch, TX: Freeman University Press.
CMS	5. Frank Martin, "Wheat and Rye," in *Earth Poems*, ed. Louise J. Cowley (North Branch, TX: Freeman University Press, 2004), 21-22. [Initial reference. See General Principles, #4, for subsequent reference patterns.]

11. Guest Author Preface, Forward, Introduction, etc.

MLA	Williams, Jane. Preface. *The Art of Vision*. By Cameron Willes. Philadelphia: Decker & Smith, 1972. Print.
APA	Williams, J. (1972). Preface. In C. Willes, *The art of vision* (pp. iii-iv). Philadelphia: Decker & Smith.
CMS	6. Jane Williams, preface to *The Art of Vision*, by Cameron Willes (Philadelphia: Decker and Smith, 1972). [Initial reference. See General Principles, #4, for subsequent reference patterns.]

12. Edition beyond the First

MLA	Lopes, Jonathan S. *Chess in the 19th Century*. 3rd ed. Chicago: Sterling, 1991. Print.
APA	Lopes, J. S. (1991). *Chess in the 19th Century* (3rd ed.). Chicago: Sterling.
CMS	7. Jonathan S. Lopes, *Chess in the 19th Century*, 3rd ed. (Chicago: Sterling, 1991), 27. [Initial reference. See General Principles, #4, for subsequent reference patterns.]

13. Book within Multivolume Set

MLA	McNally, Dan. *Gunfighters*. Ed. Jason Whalen. Vol. 2. San Francisco: Far West, 1968. Print. 3 Vols.
APA	McNally, D. (1968). In J. Whalen (Ed.), *Gunfighters: Vol. 2*. San Francisco: Far West.
CMS	8. Dan McNally, *Gunfighters*, 3 vols., ed. Jason Whalen (San Francisco: Far West, 1968), 2:341. [Initial reference. See General Principles, #4, for subsequent reference patterns.]

14. Reference Work: Encyclopedia or Dictionary

MLA	"Andalusite." *The New Encyclopedia Britannica: Micropedia.* 15th ed. 1974. Print. [If there is a named author for the reference-work entry, then that name would go before the title in the bibliographic citation. If the reference work is well-known, such as in this case, publisher name and city of publication are not needed.]
APA	Andalusite. (1974). *The new encyclopedia Britannica: Vol. 1* (15th ed.). Chicago: William Benton. [If there is a named author for the reference-work entry, then that name would go before the title in the bibliographic citation.]
CMS	9. *Encyclopedia Britannica,* 15th ed., s.v. "Andalusite." [Initial reference. See General Principles, #4, for subsequent reference patterns. If the reference work is well-known, such as in this case, publishing details beyond those given here are not needed.]

15. Corporate Author

MLA	Westerly Historical Society. *Key Dates in Glass County*. Westerly, MN: WHS Publications, 1982. Print.
APA	Westerly Historical Society. (1982). *Key dates in Glass County*. Westerly, MN: WHS Publications.
CMS	10. Westerly Historical Society, *Key Dates in Glass County* (Westerly, MN: WHS Publications, 1982), 7. [Initial reference. See General Principles, #4, for subsequent reference patterns.]

16. Sacred Text

MLA	*The New Testament of Our Lord and Savior Jesus Christ with a Comprehensive Catholic Commentary*. 1859. Ed. George L. Haydock. Monrovia, CA: Catholic Treasures, 1991. Print. Douay-Rheims Vers.
APA	*The new testament of our lord and savior Jesus Christ with a comprehensive Catholic commentary*. (1991). G. L. Haydock (Ed.). Monrovia, CA: Catholic Treasures.
CMS	11. *The New Testament of Our Lord and Savior Jesus Christ with a Comprehensive Catholic Commentary*, ed. George Leo Haydock (Monrovia, CA: Catholic Treasures, 1991), 1249.

This section exemplifies the format for physical journals, magazines, newspapers, newsletters—basically any non-electronic publication that comes out on a periodic basis, whether daily, weekly, monthly, quarterly, annually, etc..

17. Basic Journal

    a. Pagination by Volume

MLA	Sommers, Andrew. "The Three Best Proofs." *Journal of Genealogy* 16.2 (2004): 311-319. Print. [For MLA, format is the same whether paginated by volume or by issue.]
APA	Sommers, A. (2004). The three best proofs. *Journal of Genealogy, 16,* 311-319.
CMS	1. Andrew Sommers, "The Three Best Proofs," *Journal of Genealogy* 16 (2004): 311-319. [Initial reference. See General Principles, #4, for subsequent reference patterns.]

    b. Pagination by Issue

APA	Jackson, A. L. (2008). Jung's collective in practice. *Modern Psychotherapy, 38*(4), 106-122.
CMS	2. Annika L. Jackson, "Jung's Collective in Practice," *Modern Psychotherapy* 38, no. 4 (2008): 106-122. [Initial reference. See General Principles, #4, for subsequent reference patterns.]

18. Basic Magazine

a. Monthly

MLA	Bates, Frederick. "The Austrian Moment." *American Free Market* Sep. 2006: 97-104. Print.
APA	Bates, F. (2006, September). The Austrian moment. *American Free Market*, 97-104.
CMS	3. Frederick Bates, "The Austrian Moment," *American Free Market*, September 2006, 97-104. [Initial reference. See General Principles, #4, for subsequent reference patterns.]

b. Weekly

MLA	Osborne, Hal. "The Rise of Radio Spots." *Trends in Advertising* 12 Oct. 2000: 14-15. Print.
APA	Osborne, H. (2000, October 12). The rise of radio spots. *Trends in Advertising*, 14-15.
CMS	4. Hal Osborne, "The Rise of Radio Spots," *Trends in Advertising*, 12 October 2000, 14-15. [Initial reference. See General Principles, #4, for subsequent reference patterns.]

19. Newsletter

Treat newsletters as you would magazines or journals, depending on the method of sequencing used by the newsletter's publisher: volume/issue or date.

20. Basic Newspaper

MLA	Scholl, Lisa. "Homeless Numbers on the Rise." *Winston Daily News* 7 Jan. 1998: B6. Print.
APA	Scholl, L. (1998, January 7). Homeless numbers on the rise. *Winston Daily News*, p. B6.
CMS	5. Lisa Scholl, "Homeless Numbers on the Rise," *Winston Daily News*, 7 January 1998, sec. B. [Initial reference. See General Principles, #4, for subsequent reference patterns. Because there are often changes between various editions of a given issue, CMS advises not to include specific page numbers for newspaper articles.]

21. Interview

MLA	Hensley, Cole. "Words on the Road." Interview. *Alt Rock Monthly* May 2002: 19-24. Print.
APA	Hensley, C. (2002, May). Words on the road [Interview]. *Alt Rock Monthly*, 19-24.
CMS	6. Cole Hensley, "Words on the Road," interview, *Alt Rock Monthly*, May 2002, 19-24. [Initial reference. See General Principles, #4, for subsequent reference patterns.]

22. Reviews: Book, Film, Audio Recording, Performance, etc.

MLA	Marshall, Miriam. "The Great Silence." Rev. of *Plainsong*, by Lucy Graham Duncan. *North Border Quarterly* 30.3 (2007): 34. Print. [MLA follows the title of the work reviewed with the key creator of that work. For instance, if a film, then the entry would read, "dir." followed by first and last name.]
APA	Marshall, M. (2007). The great silence [Review of the book *Plainsong*]. *North Border Quarterly, 30*(3), 34.
CMS	7. Miriam Marshall, "The Great Silence," review of *Plainsong*, by Lucy Graham Duncan, *North Border Quarterly* 30, no. 3 (2007): 34. [Initial reference. See General Principles, #4, for subsequent reference patterns.]

23. Editorial

MLA	"The Far Horizon." Editorial. *Breckenridge Times* 16 Nov. 2004: A9. Print.
APA	The far horizon [Editorial]. (2004, November 16). *Breckenridge Times*, p. A9.
CMS	8. "The Far Horizon," editorial, *Breckenridge Times*, 16 November 2004, sec. A. [Initial reference. See General Principles, #4, for subsequent reference patterns.]

24. Letter to the Editor

MLA	Harkness, Sal. Letter. *Health Watch*. Dec. 1999: 4. Print.
APA	Harkness, S. (1999, December). [Letter to the editor]. *Health Watch*, p. 4.
CMS	9. Sal Harkness, letter to the editor, *Health Watch*, December 2007, 4. [Initial reference. See General Principles, #4, for subsequent reference patterns.]

Online Sources

Although the popularity of Internet research has grown quickly, it is a largely unregulated information environment, and documentation systems have had a real challenge trying to develop consistent and reliable methods of citation for online sources. Often there is no named author; rarely are there page numbers; URL's can sometimes run on for several lines; and website articles are always subject to change or elimination, so what is virtually "there" one day may not be the next. Aside from these practical problems of citation, it is often difficult to determine the origin and/or validity of a given website, which may appear to be an official and reputable source but is actually just some guy making things up from his own computer desk, stuck in a corner of his basement.

Nevertheless, the Internet seems destined both to survive and to thrive, and there are in fact a tremendous number of legitimate sources now accessible online. This section will first provide the basic sequence of citation information for each of the three major systems, and then give some specific examples of bibliographic citations for a few of the various types of online sources you are most likely to encounter.

MLA

1. Author name (corporate if individual not available)
   - If unknown author, resort first to subpage title, then to website title
2. Subpage (or article) title, in quotation marks, if available
3. Website name, in italics
4. Sponsoring organization, if any
   - If none available, use the abbreviation, N.p., for "no publisher."
5. Date of publication or last update
   - If none available, use the abbreviation, n.d., for "no date."
6. Source medium (i.e. the word, Web.)
7. Date of access (in day-month-year format)

APA

1. Author name (corporate, if individual not available)
   - If unknown author, resort first to subpage title, then to website title
2. Date of publication, in parentheses
   - If none available, use the abbreviation, n.d., for "no date."
3. Subpage (or article) title, in italics
4. Date of access (usually only if there is no publication date)
   - Format: Retrieved month-day, year
5. Digital Object Identifier (DOI) or database document number, if available
   - If not, then use direct Uniform Resource Locator (URL)

<u>CMS</u>

1. Author name (corporate, if individual not available)
   - If unknown author, use website name or site-owner name
2. Subpage (or article) title, in quotation marks
3. Website name or site owner
4. Digital Object Identifier (DOI), if available
5. Direct Uniform Resource Locator (URL)
6. Optional: access date in parentheses

25. Online Book (i.e. an entire book, readable online)

MLA	Sorenson, Luke. *Apple Tree Diseases. Ointl.org*. Organic International, 2006. Web. 14 Apr. 2007.
APA	Sorenson, L. (2006). *Apple tree diseases*. Retrieved from Organic International website, http://ointl.org/books/atd.html
CMS	1. Luke Sorenson, *Apple Tree Diseases*, Organic International, (Akron, OH: Old Wisdom Books, 2003), http://ointl.org/books/atd.html (accessed April 14, 2007). [Initial reference. See General Principles, #4, for subsequent reference patterns. Note that even for the electronic version of a book, CMS recommends corresponding print-version city and publisher information if available.]

26. Online-Periodical Article (i.e. from an online version of a journal or magazine)

Some print periodicals have a corresponding online version, and some periodicals exist only online. In either case, the bibliographic citation follows, for the most part, the format of print periodicals; in addition, each of the major systems—MLA, APA, and CMS—has a few extra details, relating to the electronic nature of the source, to add. The following example is for an online journal, so the date indication is the same as for that of a print journal. If the example were of an online magazine or newspaper, then the date details would follow those print formats accordingly.

MLA	Moreli, Susan. "A Brief History of Water Symbols." *Dream Studies*. 9.4 (2005): n. pag. Web. 22 July 2006. [For online journals without page numbers, MLA uses the abbreviation, n. pag.. Otherwise, the page range of the particular article would be included after the year.]
APA	Moreli, S. (2005). A brief history of water symbols. *Dream Studies,* 9(4). doi: 10.1006/ds.2005.0341 [If there were not a doi number, then the format would be as follows: Retrieved July 22, 2006, from http://www.drst.com/9.4/moreli.htm]
CMS	2. Susan Moreli, "A Brief History of Water Symbols," *Dream Studies* 9, no. 4 (2005), doi: 10.1006/ds.2005.0341, http://www.drst.com/9.4/moreli.htm. [Initial reference. See General Principles, #4, for subsequent reference patterns.]

27. Article from a Database

Libraries typically subscribe to very large databases, in which print articles from thousands of journals, magazines, and newspapers have been stored electronically. Often these articles are printed out and thereby become a personal copy for the researcher. Bibliographic citations for these articles follow, in general, the same guidelines as their print-version counterparts, with some additional detail relating to the database from which they were retrieved.

MLA	Willes, Joseph A. "The Same Old Maneuvering." *Washington World* 27 Oct. 2004: 24-25. *News Bank Unlimited*. Web. 11 Nov. 2008. [Note that the name of the database provider, News Bank Unlimited, is italicized.]
APA	Willes, J. A. (2004, October 27). The same old maneuvering. *Washington World,* 24-25. Retrieved November 11, 2008, from News Bank Unlimited database. [If there is no identifying document number, such as a DOI or one assigned by the database itself, then articles retrieved from a database should show the retrieval date, as in this example, but a URL is not necessary.]
CMS	3. Joseph A. Willes, "The Same Old Maneuvering," *Washington World*, 27 October 2004, 24-25, http://www.newsbankunlimited.com/. [Initial reference. See General Principles, #4, for subsequent reference patterns.]

MLA	Jones, Harmony. "The Sicilian Since the Sixties." *Modern Chess Ideas.* The International Institute of Chess Studies, n.d. Web. 12 Jan. 2009. [When there is no date of creation or last update given, MLA still marks that slot in the citation with the "n.d." (no date) designation.]
APA	Jones, H. (n.d.). *The Sicilian since the sixties.* Retrieved January 12, 2009, from Modern Chess Ideas website, http://www.modernchessideas.com/openings/sicilian.2.htm [Date of access is given here only because there is no date (or update) on the subpage article, shown here by the "n.d." (no date) designation right after the author name.]
CMS	4. Harmony Jones, "The Sicilian Since the Sixties," *Modern Chess Ideas*, The International Institute of Chess Studies, http://www.modernchessideas.com/openings/sicilian.2.htm (accessed January 12, 2009). [Initial reference. See General Principles, #4, for subsequent reference patterns. Especially since there is no publication date, the optional access (retrieval) date has been included in this example.]

MLA	Saturn5. "Re: Near-miss Asteroids." *Am-Astronomer Discussion Board.* Society of Amateur Astronomers, 2 Sep. 2002. Web. 14 Feb. 2004. [Note that the author name is a message-board "handle," or nickname. Actual author name should, of course, be used if available.]
APA	Saturn5. (2002, September 2). Near-miss asteroids. Message posted to the Am-Astronomer discussion board, http://www.saastronomers.org/db/2002/nearmissasteroids/21.html [APA cites message-board posts on the References page *only* if it is retrievable. If not, it should be treated as personal correspondence and cited only in-text. Note that the author name is a message-board "handle," or nickname. Actual author name should, of course, be used if available.]
CMS	5. Saturn5, "Near-miss Asteroids," message to *Am-Astronomer Discussion Board*, Society of Amateur Astronomers, 2 September 2002, http://www.saastronomers.org/db/2002/nearmissasteroids/21.html. [Initial reference. See General Principles, #4, for subsequent reference patterns. Note that the author name is a message-board "handle," or nickname. Actual author name should, of course, be used if available. Optional access (retrieval) date not included in this example, but note that there is an exact date for the posted source material: 2 September 2002.]

30. Comment to a Blog Posting

A weblog (or "blog") is a kind of website, so a blog post would be cited using the website format (see #28). Many blog postings, however, allow for reader comments in reaction to the posts themselves. The following examples illustrate how such comments would be cited on the bibliographic information page of each system—MLA, APA, and CMS.

MLA	Wiles, Wayman. Weblog comment. "The Vermont Shires." *Secession Watch*. N.p. 23 Aug. 2008. Web. 12 Jan. 2009. [Note that when there is not an identifiable publisher or sponsor, the designation, "N.p.," (No publisher) is used. Also note that in this case, there is an author name; often, however, in the comments section, only nicknames or screen-names are available, in which case such would be used in place of the author name.]
APA	Wiles, W. (2008, August 23). The Vermont shires. [Web log comment]. Retrieved from Secession Watch blog, http://www.secessionwatch.org/2008.8.23/vermontshires/ comm/9.html [APA cites weblog comments on the References page *only* if it is retrievable. If not, it should be treated as personal correspondence and cited only in-text. Also note that in this case, there is an author name; often, however, in the comments section, only nicknames or screen-names are available, in which case such would be used in place of the author name.]
CMS	6. Wayman Wiles, "The Vermont Shires," comment to *Secession Watch* web log, 23 August 2008, http://www.secessionwatch.org/ 2008.8.23/vermontshires/comm/9.html. [Initial reference. See General Principles, #4, for subsequent reference patterns. Note that in this case, there is an author name; often, however, in the comments section, only nicknames or screen-names are available, in which case such would be used in place of the author name. The optional date of access is not included here, but there is an exact date for the posted source material: 23 August 2008.]

31. Public Documents

a. United States Constitution (and other statutes)

MLA	[For very well-known documents, no bibliographic citation is necessary, and an in-text citation suffices—as follows, for example: (US Const. art. 2, sec. 1).]
APA	U.S. Const. Art. II, sec. 1.
CMS	7. U. S. Constitution, art. 2, sec. 1.

b. Historical Documents (appearing within another text)

MLA	Jefferson, Thomas, et al. The Declaration of Independence. 1776. *Documents Illustrative of the Formation of the Union of the American States*. Ed. Charles C. Tansill. Washington, DC: Government Printing Office, 1927. 22-26. Print.
APA	Jefferson, T. et al. (1776). The Declaration of Independence. In C. Tansill (Ed.), *Documents Illustrative of the Formation of the Union of the American States* (pp. 22-26). (1927). Washington, DC: Government Printing Office.
CMS	8. Thomas Jefferson et al., "The Declaration of Independence," in *Documents Illustrative of the Formation of the Union of the American States*, ed. Charles C. Tansill (Washington, DC: GPO, 1927), 22-26.

32. Film (e.g. motion picture, video, or DVD)

MLA	*The Last Salesman*. Dir. Thomas Harper. Perf. Karen Shay, James McFarland, and Nancy Cairns. Starlight Entertainment, 2007. Film. [The media type in this case is "Film," because it was viewed in a commercial theater. If viewed by way of a video or DVD, the media type would be "Videocassette" or "DVD," respectively.]
APA	Jacobson, R. (Producer), & Harper, T. (Director). (2007). *The last salesman* [Motion picture]. Hollywood, CA: Starlight Entertainment. [The designation, "Motion picture," is used because the film was viewed in a commercial theater. If viewed by way of a video or DVD, then use "Film" or "DVD," respectively.]
CMS	9. *The Last Salesman*, motion picture, directed by Thomas Harper (Hollywood, CA: Starlight Entertainment, 2007). [Initial reference. See General Principles, #4, for subsequent reference patterns. The designation, "motion picture," is used because the film was viewed in a commercial theater. If viewed by way of a video or DVD, then use "videocassette" or "DVD," respectively.]

33. Audio Recording (e.g. CD, cassette tape, or digital file)

MLA	Delacroix, Sam. "Moon Is Weeping." *Sunset Melodies*. Autumn Records, 1994. CD.
APA	Delacroix, S. (1994). Moon is weeping. *Sunset melodies*. [CD]. Minneapolis, MN: Autumn Records.
CMS	10. Sam Delacroix, "Moon Is Weeping," *Sunset Melodies*, compact disc, (Autumn Records, 1994). [Initial reference. See General Principles, #4, for subsequent reference patterns.]

34. Television Program

MLA	"Gatewood." *American Mansions*. Host Eleanor Strom. PBS. KRLP, Grand Meadow, MT, 9 Apr. 2002. Television.
APA	Crane, J. (Producer). (2002, April 9). Gatewood. In *American mansions*. Public Broadcasting System. Grand Meadow, MT: KRLP.
CMS	11. "Gatewood," hosted by Eleanor Strom, *American Mansions*, PBS, April 9, 2002. [Initial reference. See General Principles, #4, for subsequent reference patterns.]

35. Radio Program

MLA	*The Daily Double Take*. Host Paul Strait. NPR. KGGL, North Prairie, IA, 11 Oct. 2008. Radio.
APA	Williams, H. (Producer). (2008, October 11). *The daily double take*. National Public Radio. North Prairie, IA: KGGL.
CMS	12. Paul Strait, host, *The Daily Double Take*, NPR, October 11, 2008. [Initial reference. See General Principles, #4, for subsequent reference patterns.]

36. Public Address (e.g. speech or lecture)

MLA	Meyer, Angelo. "The Coffee Bean." Forest County High School Auditorium, Knollwood, AR. 19 Nov. 2000. Speech.
APA	Meyer, A. (2000, November 19). The coffee bean. [Speech]. Forest County High School Auditorium, Knollwood, AR.
CMS	13. Angelo Meyer, "The Coffee Bean," (speech, Forest County High School Auditorium, Knollwood, AR, November 19, 2000). [Initial reference. See General Principles, #4, for subsequent reference patterns.]

37. Live Performance (e.g. dance, drama, music)

MLA	"Spring." By Julie Tessatorie. Dir. Amy Stands. Perf. Sasza Petrov, Hans Kline. Duluth Acting Company. Wentworth Theater, Chicago. 26 Aug. 2005. Performance.
APA	Tessatorie, J. (Writer). (2005, August 26). Spring. [Play]. Wentworth Theater, Chicago.
CMS	14. Julie Tessatorie, *Spring*, (play, Wentworth Theater, Chicago, August 26, 2005). [Initial reference. See General Principles, #4, for subsequent reference patterns.]

38. Artwork

MLA	Diablo, Ray. *Moth at Candle*. 1984. Oil on canvas. Up River Art Museum, Meadowbrook, IA.
APA	Diablo, R. (1984). *Moth at candle*. [Painting]. Up River Art Museum, Meadowbrook, IA.
CMS	15. Ray Diablo, *Moth at Candle*. 1984. Oil on canvas, 24 x 36 in. Up River Art Museum, Meadowbrook, IA. [Initial reference. See General Principles, #4, for subsequent reference patterns.]

39. Personal Interview (performed by the researcher and unpublished)

MLA	Benton, Mary. Personal interview. 8 May 2006. [The designation, "personal," indicates a face-to-face interview. If by another means, such as the telephone, then "personal" would be replaced with the appropriate word.]
APA	[Since the contents of an unpublished personal interview are not publicly available, APA does not cite it on the References page but in-text only, as follows, for example: (M. Wilkins, personal communication, May 8, 2006).]
CMS	16. Mary Benton, interview by author, Chapel Bluff, North Dakota, 8 May 2006. [Initial reference. See General Principles, #4, for subsequent reference patterns.]

40. Personal Correspondence (e.g. emails, letters, conversations)

MLA	Gray, Erick. "Re: the Miller claim." Message to the author. 6 Sep. 2003. E-mail. [If a postal letter, then this format: Gray, Erick. Letter to the author. 6 Sep. 2003. TS. – where "TS" stands for typed manuscript. If handwritten, then "MS."
APA	[Since the contents of an unpublished personal correspondence are not publicly available, APA does not cite it on the References page but in-text only, as follows, for example: (E. Gray, personal correspondence, September 6, 2003).]
CMS	17. Erick Gray, email message to author, September 6, 2003. [Initial reference. See General Principles, #4, for subsequent reference patterns. If a postal letter, the "letter" would replace "email message."]

Samples of Bibliographic Information Pages

Each of the three major documentation systems—MLA, APA, and CMS—has an end-page format for listing sources used in the paper. MLA calls it the "Works Cited" page; APA calls it the "References" page; and CMS calls it, simply, "Notes." In each system, the bibliographic entries should start on a fresh page, after the text of the paper is completed. CMS also accommodates a footnote method for bibliographic citations, in which notes are placed at the bottom of the page where they appear in the text and endnotes are therefore not needed. What follows in this section are sample bibliographic pages for each documentation system.

Works Cited

Altier, Frank. "Re: New Atlantis." *Early Colonial Discussion Board.* Society for Colonial Studies,

> 2 Sep. 2008. Web. 14 Feb. 2009.

"American Frontier." *The New Encyclopedia Britannica: Micropedia.* 15th ed. 1974. Print.

Benton, Mary. Personal interview. 8 May 2006.

"The Gathering Gloom." *War Poems in Three Centuries*. Ed. Kenneth R. Mann. New York: Shore

> Brothers, 1979. Print.

Gray, Erick. "Re: the Miller claim." Message to the author. 6 Sep. 2003. E-mail.

Jacobs, Russell. "Freemasonry at the New Dawn." *Democracy Papers.com.* Frazier University,

> 14 Jun. 2003. Web. 12 Jan. 2009.

Jefferson, Thomas, et al. The Declaration of Independence. 1776. *Documents Illustrative of the*

> *Formation of the Union of the American States*. Ed. Charles C. Tansill. Washington, DC:

> Government Printing Office, 1927. 22-26. Print.

Marin, Melinda. "Timeline for the Birth of a Nation." *Key American Documents.* N.p., 2004. Web.

> 12 Jan. 2009.

Sauger, Mary. *Collected Essays of Mary Sauger*. Ed. Cheryl Berrins. New York: Crest, 1984. Print.

Wenzl, Alice. "Blueprint for Revolution." *New World History.* Nov. 2006: 43-49. Print.

---. "Reinterpreting 1789." *New World History.* Apr. 2003: 28-35. Print.

Wiles, Wayman. Weblog comment. "The Vermont Shires." *Secession Watch*. N.p. 23 Aug. 2008.

> Web. 14 Jan. 2009.

Willes, Joseph A. "The Same Old Maneuvering." *Washington World* 27 Oct. 2004: 24-25. *News*

> *Bank Unlimited*. Web. 28 Jan. 2009.

References

Altier, F. (2008, September 2). New Atlantis. Message posted to the Early Colonial discussion

    board, http://www.sfcolonials.org/db/92008/newatlantis/04.html

American frontier. (1974). *The new encyclopedia Britannica: Vol. 1* (15th ed.). Chicago: William

    Benton.

Anonymous. The gathering gloom. (1979). In K. R. Mann (Ed.), *War poems in three centuries*

    (p. 95). New York: Shore Brothers.

Jacobs, R. (2003, June 14). *Freemasonry at the new dawn.* Retrieved January 12, 2009, from

    Democracy Papers.com website, http://www.dpfu.com/14.6.2003.1.html

Jefferson, T. et al. (1776). The Declaration of Independence. In C. Tansill (Ed.), *Documents*

    Illustrative of the Formation of the Union of the American States (pp. 22-26). (1927).

    Washington, DC: Government Printing Office.

Marin, M. (2004). *Timeline for the birth of a nation.* doi: 10.1421/kad.2004.08

Sauger, M. (1984). In C. Berrins (Ed.), *Collected essays of Mary Sauger.* New York: Crest.

Wenzl, A. (2003, April). Reinterpreting 1789. *New World History*, 28-35.

Wenzl, A. (2006, November). Blueprint for revolution. *New World History*, 43-49.

Wiles, W. (2008, August 23). The Vermont shires. [Web log comment]. Retrieved from Secession

    Watch blog, http://www.secessionwatch.org/2008.8.23/vermontshires/comm/9.html

Willes, J. A. (2004, October 27). The same old maneuvering. *Washington World,* 24-25. Retrieved

    November 11, 2008, from News Bank Unlimited database.

Notes

1. Alice Wenzl, "Blueprint for Revolution," *New World History*, November, 2006, 43-49.

2. Ibid., 47.

3. Alice Wenzl, "Reinterpreting 1789," *New World History*, April, 2003, 28-35.

4. Wenzl, "Blueprint," 48.

5. "The Gathering Gloom," in *War Poems in Three Centuries*, ed. Kenneth R. Mann (New York: Shore Brothers, 1979), 95.

6. Mary Sauger, *Collected Essays of Mary Sauger*, ed. Cheryl Berrins (New York: Crest, 1984), 72.

7. *Encyclopedia Britannica*, 15th ed., s.v. "American frontier."

8. Sauger, 72.

9. Ibid.

10. Russell Jacobs, "Freemasonry at the New Dawn," *Democracy Papers.com*, Frazier University, http://www.dpfu.com/14.6.2003.1.html (accessed January 12, 2009).

11. Ibid.

12. Ibid.

13. Wayman Wiles, "The Vermont Shires," comment to *Secession Watch* web log, 23 August 2008, http://www.secessionwatch.org/2008.8.23/vermontshires/comm/9.html.

14. Frank Altier, "Re: New Atlantis," message to *Early Colonial Discussion Board*, Society for Colonial Studies, 2 September 2008, http://www.sfcolonials.org/db/92008/newatlantis/04.html.

15. Thomas Jefferson et al., "The Declaration of Independence," in *Documents Illustrative of the Formation of the Union of the American States*, ed. Charles C. Tansill (Washington, DC: GPO, 1927), 22-26.

16. Ibid, 25.

17. Wiles, "Vermont Shires."

18. Mary Benton, interview by author, Chapel Bluff, North Dakota, 8 May 2006.

19. Erick Gray, email message to author, September 6, 2003.

20. Benton interview.

21. Melinda Marin, "Timeline for the Birth of a Nation," *Key American Documents*, 2004, doi: 10.1421/kad.2004.08, http://www.keyamericandocs.com/Timeline/birth.html.

22. Joseph A. Willes, "The Same Old Maneuvering," *Washington World*, 27 October 2004, 24-25, http://www.newsbankunlimited.com/.

Sample of CMS Footnote Style

… Historian Alice Wenzl argues persuasively that revolutionary plans were in place as much as a decade before the actual revolution took place.[1] She refers specifically to the Hartel Papers, discovered recently in a private library, as being the strongest piece of evidence.[2] She had put forth this same basic assertion about the pre-planning of the American Revolution several years prior but without the help of this latest discovery.[3] The undeniable implication of her argument, if true, is that the American Revolution was not—nor are perhaps any revolutions—spontaneous acts.[4] …

---

1. Alice Wenzl, "Blueprint for Revolution," *New World History*, November, 2006, 43-49.
2. Ibid., 47.
3. Alice Wenzl, "Reinterpreting 1789," *New World History*, April, 2003, 28-35.
4. Wenzl, "Blueprint," 48.

Appendix

Key Documentation Resources

MLA

Style Guide: *MLA Handbook for Writers of Research Papers*. 7th Edition.

Website: www.mlahandbook.org

APA

Style Guide: *Publication Manual of the American Psychological Association*. 6th Edition.

Website: www.apastyle.org

CMS

Style Guide: The Chicago Manual of Style. 15th Edition.

Website: www.chicagomanualofstyle.org

Other Discipline-Specific Organizations with Style Guidelines

CSE – Council of Science Editors (www.councilscienceeditors.org)

APSA – American Political Science Association (www.apsanet.org)

ASA – American Sociological Association (www.asanet.org)

ASCE – American Society of Civil Engineers (www.asce.org)

About the Author

Michael Larson teaches English at Minnesota State College – Southeast Technical, in Winona, Minnesota. He holds a Master of Fine Arts degree in Creative Writing and a Master of Arts degree in English Literature. He is the author of a book of poems, *What We Wish We Knew*, a chapbook of poems, *The Light Remaining*, and two forthcoming textbooks, *Durable Design: Classical Oration for Speeches and Essays* and *English Grammar Tables: A Concise Visual Reference*. Mr. Larson is also the recipient of a National Endowment for the Arts fellowship in poetry, a Loft-McKnight fellowship in poetry, and an Iowa State Arts Board grant in fiction.

Made in the USA
San Bernardino, CA
08 September 2014